THE GREEN WAVE

MURIEL RUKEYSER

The Green Wave

DOUBLEDAY & COMPANY, INC.

Garden City   1948   New York

WGE

FOR

MARIE de L. WELCH

I wish to thank the Guggenheim Foundation for a fellowship which helped with the time of this book, a play, and poems in my book Beast in View.

Let poems and bodies love and be given to air,
Earth having us real in her seasons, our fire and savor;
And, reader, love well, imagine forward, for
All of the testaments are in your favor.

Some of these poems have appeared in Kenyon Review, Poetry, Twice a Year, Tomorrow, *and the* California Poetry Folios. *The play,* The Middle of the Air, *was produced in Iowa City in 1945 by Hallie Flanagan.*

CONTENTS

THE GREEN WAVE

WATER NIGHT

The sky behind the farthest shore
Is darker than I go to sleep.

Blackness of water, the crater at the core,
The many blacknesses begin to gleam.

Rivers of darkness bind me to this land
While overhead the moon goes far to shine,

And now nothing nobody is my own.
The motion of streams glitters before my eyes:

Sources and entrances, they lie no more,
Now darkly keep, now flow now bright

Until all wandering end, a hand
Shine, and the leadings homeward of delight

Seem to begin my deepest sleep
To make a lake of dream.

EYES OF NIGHT-TIME

On the roads at night I saw the glitter of eyes:
my dark around me let shine one ray;   that black
allowed their eyes   :   spangles in the cat's, air in the moth's
    eye shine,
mosaic of the fly, ruby-eyed beetle, the eyes that never weep,
the horned toad sitting and its tear of blood,
fighters and prisoners in the forest, people
aware in this almost total dark, with the difference,
the one broad fact of light.

Eyes on the road at night, sides of a road like rhyme;
the floor of the illumined shadow sea
and shallows with their assembling flash and show
of sight, root, holdfast, eyes of the brittle stars.
And your eyes in the shadowy red room,
scent of the forest entering, various time
calling and the light of wood along the ceiling
and over us birds calling and their circuit eyes.
And in our bodies the eyes of the dead and the living
giving us gifts at hand, the glitter of all their eyes.

THIS PLACE IN THE WAYS

Having come to this place
I set out once again
on the dark and marvelous way
from where I began:
belief in the love of the world,
woman, spirit, and man.

Having failed in all things
I enter a new age
seeing the old ways as toys,
the houses of a stage
painted and long forgot;
and I find love and rage.

Rage for the world as it is
but for what it may be
more love now than last year
and always less self-pity
since I know in a clearer light
the strength of the mystery.

And at this place in the ways
I wait for song.
My poem-hand still, on the paper,
all night long.
Poems in throat and hand, asleep,
and my storm beating strong!

SONG, FROM
"MR. AMAZEEN ON THE RIVER"

Over the water, where I lie alive,
   Grass burns green where the buried are,
   Tall stone is standing   "And the sea
   Gave up its dead."   The wave, the living star,
   Evening and house at river-mouth shine.

The hour of voices on the water and oars
   Speaking of blue, speaking of time.
   His colors, colors of deepness will arrive,
   Island-sleep, keel-sleep, cloud-controlling evening.
   They say to me at last "I am your home."

CLOUDS, AIRS, CARRIED ME AWAY

Clouds, airs, carried me away,
but here we stand
and newborn we begin.
Having seen all the people of the play,
the lights, the map in the hand,
we know there will be wars
all acted out, and know not who may win.

Deep now in your great eyes, and in my gross
flesh — heavy as ever, woman of mud—
shine sunset, sunrise and the advancing stars.
But past all loss
and all forbidding a thing is understood.

Orpheus in hell remembered rivers
and a music rose
full of all human voices;
all words you wish are in that living sound.
And even torn to pieces
one piece sang
Come all ye torn and wounded here
together
and one sang to its brother
remembering.
One piece in tatters sang among its blood:
man is a weapon, woman's a trap;
and so is the hand with the map, my dear,
so is the hand with the colored map.
And I to myself the tightest trap.

23

Now all is young again:
in a wet night among the household music,
the new time,
by miracle my traps are sprung.
I wished you all your good again
and all your good is here with you,
smiling, various, and true,
your living friends, as live as we.

I believed because I saw not;
now I see,
with love become
so haunted by a living face
that all the dead rise up and stare;
and the dumb time, the year that was
passes away.   Memory is reborn,
form and forgiveness shine.
So in this brilliant dark, dark of the year,
shining is born.
We know what we do,
and turn, and act in hope.
Now the wounds of time
have healed and are grown.
They are not wounds, they are mine,
they are healed into mouths.
They speak past wrongs.   I am born;
you bring shining, and births.
Here are the stories they tell you,
here are their songs.

SALAMANDER

Red leaf.   And beside it, a red leaf alive
flickers, the eyes set wide in the leaf head,
small broad chest, a little taper of flame for tail
moving a little among the leaves like fear.

Flickering red in the wet week of rain
while a bird falls safely through his mile of air.

HIS HEAD IS FULL OF FACES

for Bernard Perlin

Now he has become one who upon that coast
landed by night and found the starving army.
Fed on their cheese and wine.   In those ravines
hidden by orphaned furious children lay
while cries and wounds and hour past hour of war
flamed past the broken pillars of that sky.

He saw the enemy.   His head is full of faces—
the living, the brave, a pure blazing alone
to fight a domination to the end.
And now he sees the rigid terrible friend
inert, peopled by armies, winning.   Now
he has become one given his life by those
fighting in Greece forever under a star
and now he knows how many wars there are.

MRS. WALPURGA

In wet green midspring, midnight and the wind
floodladen and ground-wet, and the immense dry moon.
Mrs. Walpurga under neon saw
the fluid airs stream over fluid evening,
ground, memory, give way and rivers run
into her sticky obsessive kiss of branches,
kiss of a real and visionary mouth,
the moon, the mountain, the round breast's sleepless eye.

Shapes of her fantasy in music from the bars,
swarming like juke-box lights the avenues;
no longer parked in the forest, from these cars,
these velvet rooms and wooden tourist camps,
sheetless under the naked white of the moon.
Wet gaze of eye, plum-color shadow and young
streams of these mouths, the streaming surface of earth
flowing alive with water, the egg and its becoming.

Coming in silence.   The shapes of every dread
seducing the isolated will.   They do not care.
They are not tortured, not tired, not alone.
They break to an arm, a leg, half of a mouth,
kissing disintegrate, flow whole, couple again;
she is changed along, she is a stream in a stream.

These are her endless years, woman and child, in dream
molded and wet, a bowl growing on a wheel,
not mud, not bowl, not clay, but this *becoming,*
winter and split of darkness, years of wish.
To want these couples, want these coupling pairs,
emblems of many parents, of the bed,
of love divided by dream, love with his dead wife,
love with her husband dead, love with his living love.

Mrs. Walpurga cries out : "It is not true!"
The light shifts, flowing away.   "It was never like——"
She stops, but nothing stops.   It moves.   It moves.
And not like anything.   And it is true.
The shapes disfigure.   Here is the feature man,
not whole, he is detail, he gleams and goes.
Here is the woman all cloth, black velvet face,
black, head to ground, close black fit to the skin,
slashed at the mouth and eyes, slashed at the breasts,
slashed at the triangle, showing rose everywhere.

Nights are disturbed, here is a crying river
running through years, here is the flight among
all the Objects of Love.   This wish, this gesture
irresisted, immortal seduction!   The young sea
streams over the land of dream, and there
the mountain like a mist-flower, the dark upright peak.
And over the sheet-flood Mrs. Walpurga
in whitened cycles of her changing moon.

28

The silence and the music change;   this song
rises and sharps, and never quite can scream—
but this is laughter harsher than nakedness
can take — in the shady shady grove the leaves
move over, the men and women move and part,
the river braids and unfolds in mingling song;
and here is the rain of summer from the moon,
relenting, wet, and giving life at last,
and Mrs. Walpurga and we may wake.

A CERTAIN MUSIC

Never to hear, I know in myself complete
that naked integrated music;   now
it has become me, now it is nerve, song, gut,
and my gross hand writes only through Mozart;   see
even in withholding what you have brought to me.

Renewed, foolish, reconciled to myself, I walk
this winter-country, I fly over its still-flock'd clouds,
always in my isolated flesh I take
that theme's light certainty of absolute purpose
to make quick spirit when spirit most might break.

Naked you walked through my body and I turned
to you with this far music you now withhold.
O my destroyed hope!   Though I never again
hear developing heaven, the growing grave-bearing earth,
my poem, my promise, my love, my sleep after love;
my hours, listening, along that music move,
and have been saved and hardly know the cold.

THE MOTIVE OF ALL OF IT

The motive of all of it was loneliness,
All the panic encounters and despair
Were bred in fear of the lost night, apart,
Outlined by pain, alone.   Promiscuous
As mercy.   Fear-led and led again to fear
At evening toward the cave where part fire, part
Pity lived in that voluptuousness
To end one and begin another loneliness.

This is the most intolerable motive :   this
Must be given back to life again,
Made superhuman, made human, out of pain
Turned to the personal, the pure release:
The rings of Plato and Homer's golden chain
Or Lenin with his cry of Dare We Win.

GREEN LIMITS

My limits crowd around me
like years, like those I loved
whose narrow hope could never
carry themselves.

My limits stand beside me
like those two widowed aunts
who from an empty beach
tore me into the wave.

Green over my low head
the surf threw itself down
tall as my aunts whose hands
locked me past help.

The sand was far behind
and rushing underfoot
water and fear and childhood,
surf of love.

Green limits walled me, water
stood higher than I saw—
glass walls, fall back!   let me
dive and be saved.

My limits stand inside me
forever like that wave
on which I ride at last
over and under me.

THE CHILDREN'S ORCHARD

In the full sun.   In the fruitfall season.
Against my knees the earth and the bucket, and the soft blue prunes
echoing red   echoing purple   echoing in the silver bucket
sun, and over the flames of earth the sun flies down.

Over my head the little trees tremble alive in their black branches
and bare-ribbed boys golden and shouting stoop here to gather the
      blue,
the wild-red, the dark.   Colors of ripeness in the fruitfall season.
I will remember the last light on the lowest branch.

Will see these trees as they were in spring, wild black rooted in light,
root-deep in noon, the piercing yellow noon of mustard-blossom.
Sun breathing on us the scent of heat, richness of air where my
      hands know
blue, full summer, strong sun.   I tell you harvest.

CHRISTMAS EVE

The secret child walks down the street
of the year's winter black and white,
while evening flames, blue-green and high—
the smooth face turns in the snow-smooth street
to lights, star-bubbles, the dark tree,
the giant star in the sacred sky.

Children behind their windows sing
a cradle, a birth, the pilgrim kings,
praising the still and wild.
They praise the face, the quickening,
the various joy, the wound!   They sing
a new prophetic child.

Out of the street, out of the spire,
a slow voice, radio or king,
begins above the mystery.
Tells pain and sweetness, pain and fire.
The bells begin to cast their rings
of celebration down the sky.

The secret child walks down the street
of needle-dark December smells.
She walks with wonder everywhere.
Who is that Child?   Where is that sweet
face of the songs and silver bells,
the broad red saint, the angelhair?

The voice tells ragged ships that sailed
to find that birth and piercèd hand,
a little child among the Jews.
"But I," she says, "I am a child
of Jews—"   Says, "This is Christianland
and things are otherwise.

"People, beasts, and a winter rose,
procession and thorn, the suffering
that had to be, the needed loss
led to this flame among the snows.
Three agents brought about this thing:
the Father, the Jews, the blessèd cross.

"And one of these is ours and overhead;
and one is God;   and one is still outside."
Sure of the birth then, the people all went to sleep.
But the child was awake, and grieved for the time ahead,
awake all night, watching the land and the sky.
Did the child weep?   No the child did not weep.

CRAYON HOUSE

Two or three lines across;   the black ones, down,
into the ground where grass sparkles and shines;
but the foundation is the green and the shine.
Windows are drawn in.   Overhead the sun
surrounded by his crown, continually given.
It is a real place, door, floor, and windows.

I float past it.   I look in at the little children.
I climb up the straight and planted path, alone.
In the city today grown, walking on stone,
a suddenness of doors, windows, bread and rolls.

Roads are in all I know   :   weapon and refugee,
color of thunder calling   Leave this room,
Get out of this house.   Even then, joy began,
went seeking through the green world, wild and no longer wild,
always beginning again.   Steady giving and green decision,
and the beginning was real.   The drawing of a child.

A CHARM FOR CANTINFLAS

After the lights and after the rumba and after the bourbon
                    and after the beer
and after the drums and after the samba and after the
                    ice cream and not long after
failure, loss, despair, and loss and despair
There was the laughter and there was Cantinflas at last
                    and his polka
doing the bumps with a hot guitar
turning unique.   Slow.   Slow.   Slow.   Deprecating
                    shoulder up.
                    Hand up.
                    All the fingers tall.
Panache and rags and triumph and smile—
beggar of light in ridiculous sunlight.

All things human clumsy and fair
as graceful as loving as stupid as true.

And on this floor
the dancers, in this square the little trees,
and on this stage always the clown of our living
gives us our sunlight and our incantation
as sun does, laughing, shining, reciting dawn, noon, and down,
making all delight and healing all ills
like faraway words on jars, the labels in Protopapas' window:
marshmallow, myrtle, peppermint, pumpkin, sesame, sesame, squills.

TRADITIONAL TUNE

After the revolution came the Fuehrer;
And after the resurrection, the Christian Era.
Not yet simple and not yet free.

Just after the Exodus, in the divided sea
The chariots drowned, and then the tempering
By forty sandy years of misery.

And after the King of the Jews came Godfrey King;
Kneedeep in blood the children wandering,
Holy Holy Holy hear the children sing.

Now mouthdeep nosedeep the fires reach our eye.
Teach us from torment to fly and not to fly.
Not yet safe, not ready to die.

Illumination and night cast on the eyes of those
Believing and fighting, playing the Worldly Fool,
Fool of Thy Word, who feel the century

Rule, under whose deep wave explosion waits;
We know the dead power of Thy Allied States.
Not yet simple and not yet free.

Sailing, remembering the rock and the child,
Sailing remember the sand, the city, the wild
Holy songs.   Deaths!   Pillar of cloud and sun,

Remember us and remember them and all
Not safe, not free sailing again upon
The sacred dangerous harbor, Jerusalem.

FOGHORN IN HORROR

I know that behind these walls is the city, over these rooftops is the
    sun.
But I see black clothes only and white clothes with the fog running in
and all their shadows.
Every minute the sound of the harbor
intruding on horror with a bellow of horror:
blu-a!   blu-aa!   Ao. . . .

I try to write to you, but here too I meet failure.
It has a face like mine.
Silence and in me and over the water
only the bellowing,
Niobe howling for her life and her children.
Did you think this sorrow of women was a graceful thing?
Horrible Niobe down on her knees:
Blu-a!   Blu-aa!   Ao. . . .

Thirty years, and my full strength, and all I touch has failed.
I sit and see
the black clothes on the line are beautiful, the sky drifting away.
The white clothes of the fog beyond me, beautiful, and the shadows.
Blu-aa!   Blu-aa!   AO.

SUMMER, THE SACRAMENTO

To this bridge the pale river and flickers away in images of blue.
And is gone.   While behind me the stone mountains
stand brown with blue lights;   at my right shoulder standing
Shasta, in summer standing, blue with her white lights
near a twilight summer moon, whiter than snow
where the light of evening changes among these legends.

Under me islands lie green, planted with green feathers,
green growing, shadowy grown, gathering streams of the green trees.
A hundred streams full of shadows and your upland source
pulled past sun-islands, green in this light as grace,
risen from your sun-mountains where your voices go
returning to water and music is your face.

Flows to the flower-haunted sea, naming and singing, under my eyes
coursing, the day of the world.   And the time of my spirit streams
before me, slow autumn colors, the cars of a long train;
earth-red, earth-orange, leaf, rust, twilight of earth
stream past the evening river and over into the dark of north,
stream slow like wishes continuing toward those snows.

SPEECH OF THE MOTHER, FROM "THE MIDDLE OF THE AIR"

Act I, Sc. 4.   She is lit, standing high, with the lit line of Anne's
sleeping body at her knee.   Darkness around.
Her soliloquy will indicate the passage of a year.

A year passes behind me.   Shadows grow larger.   Time dissolves
to a moment.   I look to my children.   They change.   A smile, a
brush of the lips against my heart;   things brighten and vanish into
a kind of joy, a kind of light.
Chaos began us, war in my own time, war in my children's time,
irrevocable accusation!   I have heard the music of the sounds of
peace:
music of rivers, of street-corners, of our South,
blues, harvest-songs;   and in the faces of lovers
seen all our challenge shining as a sign
to shape the future in love and birth.
Women standing in their houses set around with order —
the bread, the doorways and tables of everyday living
through all the walls have heard the shouts of fighting,
planes in the air,
and a shrill cry of women tortured under time,
each one carrying loss like conception : a lover gone,
or a son, or her brothers disappeared.   One saying, "Spain! Spain!"
One desolate for her unborn children.   One standing alone
outside of lighted windows, or black against raving fires
of this year and next year.

Chaos began us, a people skillful in war, young in love,
and in peace unbegun.   A people various as life
whose strength is in our many voices and our hope
of a future of many, each singing his own song.
For we know this struggle   :   more than forces in conflict,
we know it as always the rising changing shadow of a dream.
A woman moving in my own house among my daughters,
I remember their hands when they were little, and smoothing
their shining hair.   They change.   And one will have her child.
                    The year passes.   Around me chaos grows.
    And darkly
our time renews itself.   And equilibrium, the healer, the young one,
the beginning of new life, poises itself on war.   And life
moves in its sharpened color into another year.
As I grow old, I face the strange seasons, I rejoice in the young,
and I say, in suffering, in joy, among the marvelous changes,
                among the accusations, all things glow.

THEN I SAW WHAT THE CALLING WAS

All the voices of the wood called "Muriel!"
but it was soon solved;   it was nothing, it was not for me.
The words were a little like Mortal and More and Endure
and a word like Real, a sound like Health or Hell.
Then I saw what the calling was   :   it was the road I traveled, the clear
time and these colors of orchards, gold behind gold and the full
shadow behind each tree and behind each slope.   Not to me
the calling, but to anyone, and at last I saw   :   where
the road lay through sunlight and many voices and the marvel
orchards, not for me, not for me, not for me.
I came into my clear being;   uncalled, alive, and sure.
Nothing was speaking to me, but I offered and all was well.

And then I arrived at the powerful green hill.

TRANSLATIONS

SIX POEMS BY OCTAVIO PAZ

Octavio Paz was born in Mexico in 1914. His collected works (1935–41) appeared in 1942; after a while in this country, he is now with the Mexican Embassy at Paris. These translations are by Octavio Paz and Muriel Rukeyser.

I The Bird

Silence of the air, of the light, of sky.
In this transparent silence
day was resting:
the transparency of space
was silence's transparency.
Motionless light of the sky was slowing
the growth of the grass.
Small things of earth, among the stones,
under identical light, were stone.
Time was sated in a minute.
And in the absorbed stillness
Noonday consumed itself.

And a bird sang, slender arrow.
The wounded silver breast shivered the sky,
the leaves moved,
and grass awoke.
And I knew that death was an arrow
who cannot know the finger on the string
and in the flicker of an eye we die.

II Poet's Epitaph

He sang until his death
singing to close his eyes
to his true life, his real life of lies;
and to remember till he died
how it had lied, his unreal life of truth.

III Spark

Sparks of fishes
in the night of the sea
and birds, sparks
in the forest night.
Our bones are sparks
in the night of the flesh.
O world, night everywhere,
the spark being life.

IV Two Bodies

Two bodies face to face
are at times two waves
and night is an ocean.

Two bodies face to face
are at times two stones
and night is a desert.

Two bodies face to face
are at times two knives
and night strikes sparks.

Two bodies face to face
are at times two roots
and night is the earth.

Two bodies face to face
are two stars falling down
in an empty sky.

V The Street

Here is a long and silent street.
I walk in blackness and I stumble and fall
and rise, and I walk blind, my feet
trampling the silent stones and the dry leaves.
Someone behind me also tramples, stones, leaves:
if I slow down, he slows;
if I run, he runs.   I turn : nobody.
Everything dark and doorless,
only my steps aware of me,
I turning and turning among these corners
which lead forever to the street
where nobody waits for, nobody follows me,
where I pursue a man who stumbles
and rises and says when he sees me : nobody.

VI Lovers

Lying in the grass
girl and boy.
Eating oranges, exchanging kisses
like waves exchanging whiteness.

Lying on the beach
girl and boy.
Eating apples, exchanging kisses
like clouds exchanging whiteness.

Lying underground
girl and boy.
Saying nothing, never kissing,
exchanging silence for silence.

RARI FROM THE MARQUESAS

The rari, or love-chant—as Samuel Elbert has pointed out—is now a museum-piece revived only on July 14. Until 1925, it was the popular song, the poetry, of the Marquesas; but it was fought relentlessly by the missionaries because of the "erotic symbolism of some of the words."

Rari *means tie or bind, love spell.* Rari kou fau *means love spells accompanied by hibiscus batons. The vocabulary of these poems is a picture language, like those of the American Indians. The images are clear, but interchangeable. Samuel Elbert speaks of the use of "mists gathering about a mountain" for a person garlanded with leis; of the following words for "lovers": night-moths, birds, mists, mountain, wreaths; of these male images: root, comet, sun, stick, fruit-pole, trade-winds; and these female images: glittering leaf, garland of red pandanus keys, fruit, bud, flower, sea-shell conch.*

The ancient chants were simple and direct: "A god constant as sunlight is her lover . . . "

"The leading poet" of the nineteenth century "was Moa Tetua." He was a blind leper who could neither read nor write; he was so popular as a composer-poet that "natives gathered illegally every night outside the leprosarium to listen" to these songs. He sings of the loves of his son, Piu, he sings stories brought to the wall by lovers and those who mourn love.

The first four rari are by Moa Tetua. The others are later.

These translations are by Samuel Elbert and Muriel Rukeyser.

These songs are like the songs that Melville heard.

55

I Rari for Tahia and Piu

by Moa Tetua

The dream-image fades, with its red pandanus keys
Strung with leaves, wet in the small rain!
He is a handsome garland.
Tahia's mouth is brave, but her eyes tremble at the spring.
Desire aroused for the valley-side boy,
Bringing the gifts of a valiant husband,
A rare fan of speckled feathers
And the loin-cloth.

Come and find the fruit!
Hold your breath!
Pressed close to my lover in the mountain,
Hidden away like children, he and I
Until the shadows of the sun climb past the mountain-top.
The *kawa* leaves have risen high toward me!
Climb the high tree, break off, O Piu,
The branch of the treasure.
Swing over the precipice we call Flowers-at-the-Peak.
My garland makes my lover happy.
Lightning flashes on the mountain flowers
Like my eyes calling you
To sleep in shame at the house of songs.
For the first time, you see the ripe and lovely fruit.
I also have seen you before, while you were tabu.

When I lay down with the chief, the sun was hot,
Handsome, you came along the stream,
My chief, my love, my soul, my palm-leaf,
My shining leaf. Farewell. The cloth is wet with tears,
    mucus and tears.
I am wet, swollen and wet and left alone.
You are away on the far, silent river.

II Rari for O'Otua

by Moa Tetua

The sun climbs, hot and burning overhead
And they return, deep in me, thoughts of love.
I sail a surf-board, landing on your shore,
And my soul walks toward you, stops.   I startle you.
In the night, it is good for man to be unwed,
We are locked together till dawn is on the sea.
The last day, when I have to go, we weep.
I cannot take my eyes from your tattooing.
My garlands, my potent fruit-plucking pole, go down to the shadows.
—You are the virile one, scented with oils, the lover.
Pick my flower, O'otua.
Kiss the superb wide-awake flower,
It is love burning in my heart.
Cut it . . . hurry up the path!
My hand, haphazard, crushes the whiteness of love.
My opened clothes were torn like this, and the clasps.

III A True Confession

by Moa Tetua

A true confession!
My love is gone in an earth-clinging rainbow!
She is gone!   My eyes are blind with tears, mist before mountains,
The sea grows smaller, feebler,
And rain pours down indeed.
My tears flow from the prison
I dream of the after-life and of my love.
The sea of my sweetheart is at low tide,
Love in my heart.
Then dawn-clouds come, the clouds dear to the god,
Great clouds rise up, up to the source of love.
Two lovers parted, and my finished dream.
The surf rises, I am held fast, taken,
Held fast, flung away, cast out on coral reefs.
Into the depths, roar upon roar!

IV Careful of the Day

by Moa Tetua

Care for love tenderly, it is deep in me.
Be careful of the day when you are old,
And old, the garlands are gone and the love-making.
Can you forget
The day we wandered into the strange cave
When we were lost?
The moon was new;
When we were parted from each other
There was only hunger.   —
I turn my head,
My head is in the shadow of a high-standing flower.
I know my real food.

V   Rari for Hepuheku

by Puko'i

O my singing lover
Bringing strength and love.
O my singing lover
Bring me a child!
Uncover the Chinese cloth!

O my singing lover,
I gave you a hat and a garland
Of vanilla flowers,
Half-opened laurel blossoms,
Half-opened laurel blossoms,
Half-opened laurel flowers!

Come, gardenia of Tahiti,
Strike with the rice-white weapon,
Into heaven twist and turn
The circumcised end—
Raise the blue flower!

VI Rari

by Taman

I wear a garland and take my beloved's hand,
Dewdrops are in my song, dewdrops.
A gift of a wreath, a gift of peace.

Strong fires disturb her, the girl is mad with love.
My thoughts are sad, in the cruel mists and mountains.
I weep as I make my clothes.　　I sing.　　Why has he gone?

I wear a garland of seven-petaled flowers.
The mountains are our love, the sky our clothing,
And wreaths our destruction.

VII Rari to Encourage Youth

by Kahu' Einui

When a man's body is young
At night he gives up his sleep
And sings, and sings!

Lovesick, with the singing sickness,
With the dizzy sickness,
When even earth and clouds flame with desire!

Chorus.   Until the body is like an old woman,
Like an eel in a hole in the sea,
Pounding, pounding!

VIII   Rari, to be Bothered by Mosquitoes

by Te'i'i Puei

Here's the story, my darling, of the dancing flower.
Song of nothing, song of nothing at all.
What about it?

Chorus.   How can I stay alone?
              How can I live alone?
              How can I love alone?
              How can I sing alone?

From Sombre-water came the love
I dreamed of in the night.
Until the cock crowed I had my joy,
And I sweated.

My lover is carried on currents of the sea!
And I stay to sleep alone,
Bothered by mosquitoes,
And sleeping all alone!

IX Not Before I Fall Asleep

The clouds are dark
Above the mountain-top —
The sweet-smelling skin
Of my love, and her gay garlands!
O not too soon, not too soon,
Not before I fall asleep. . . .

Chorus.   You desire me!   You love me!
You make me fall with you in a comet.
A song, a song.
For your brow a wreath and a song.

EASTER EVE

1945

EASTER EVE 1945

Wary of time O it seizes the soul tonight
I wait for the great morning of the west
confessing with every breath mortality.
Moon of this wild sky struggles to stay whole
and on the water silvers the ships of war.
I go alone in the black-yellow light
all night waiting for day, while everywhere the sure
death of light, the leaf's sure return to the root
is repeated in million, death of all man to share.
Whatever world I know shines ritual death,
wide under this moon they stand gathering fire,
fighting with flame, stand fighting in their graves.
All shining with life as the leaf, as the wing shines,
the stone deep in the mountain, the drop in the
                    green wave.
Lit by their energies, secretly, all things shine.
Nothing can black that glow of life;   although
                    each part go crumbling down
                    itself shall rise up whole.

Now I say there are new meanings;   now I name
death our black honor and feast of possibility
to celebrate casting of life on life.   This earth-long day
between blood and resurrection where we wait
remembering sun, seed, fire;   remembering
that fierce Judaean Innocent who risked
every immortal meaning on one life.
Given to our year as sun and spirit are,
as seed we are blessed only in needing freedom.
Now I say that the peace the spirit needs is peace,
not lack of war, but fierce continual flame.
For all men   :   effort is freedom, effort's peace,
it fights.   And along these truths the soul goes home,
     flies in its blazing to a place
     more safe and round than Paradise.

Night of the soul, our dreams in the arms of dreams
dissolving into eyes that look upon us.
Dreams the sources of action, the meeting and the end,
a resting-place among the flight of things.
And love which contains all human spirit, all wish,
the eyes and hands, sex, mouth, hair, the whole woman —
fierce peace I say at last, and the sense of the world.
In the time of conviction of mortality
whatever survive, I remember what I am. —
The nets of this night are on fire with sun and moon
pouring both lights into the open tomb.
Whatever arise, it comes in the shape of peace,
fierce peace which is love, in which move all the stars,
and the breathing of universes, filling, falling away,
and death on earth cast into the human dream.

   What fire survive forever
   myself is for my time.

PRIVATE LIFE OF THE SPHINX

PRIVATE LIFE OF THE SPHINX

for Ella Winter

I

Simply because of a question, my life is implicated:
my flesh and answer fly between chaos and their need.
On the rock I asked the shaky king
one foolish question to make him look at himself —
He looked.   Beheld himself and kingdoms.   Took.
My claws and smile transferred into his myth.

Babble of demand, and answers building the brilliant cities
the standing battlefields and the fields of the fallen down.

Now in this city in the Lounge of Time,
I tell you it was a legend founded on fire,
founded on what we are.   Simply because I asked one question,
"What is this, What?"   so that the answer must be "Man."
Because of that they bring their riddles and rhyme
to my door if I houseless run throughout the world,
torse of a woman and quarters of a lion.

II

Open war with its images of love and death —
man, an explosion walking through the night in
rich and intolerable loneliness.
Cathedrals writhing gold against their clouds
and a child asking the fiery pure questions.
The monkey-dark, a month of smoky violets,
delicate repose of my reality among
dreams, and the angel of the resurrection,
a mouth overhead, the sky planted with stars.

My questions are my body.   And among this glowing, this sure,
this fact, this mooncolored breast, I make memorial.

III

My body is set against disorder.   Risen among enigmas,
time and the question carry a rose of form,
sing a life-song.   Strangler and bitch, they said,
but they mistook the meaning of my name:
I am the root who embraces and the source.
I sing.   I sing.

In these cities, all suffer from their weaknesses—
they lack some gut, they are ill, they have womb-envy,
run howling from the question and the act.
They bring me their need for answers in their hands and eyes.
To embody truth, the Irish old man said.

I remember in Calabria a peasant
broad, smiling, and sly, with a bird throbbing and small
behind his back, in his hands;   and he asked his question.
Is it alive? and he smiled at me.   Then I knew
if I said Yes, he would twist the sparrow's neck.
The fool of time!   I gave him my only answer,
that answer of time:
Fool, I said, you know it depends on you
whether it live or die.

IV

I answer!   I fly reborn from deep escape!
Listen to their cries, the selfsame crying throats,
crying the selfsame need.
Here is my self.   I touch you, life reaches me.
You touch me, I am able to give my gifts.
All the acts flow together, a form being made.
I know a garden beyond questioning—
can almost see night-flowering white mallows,
can almost tell you below the sound of water,
white lilac like a voluptuous light
shining at full on our two faces —
It goes ahead of our hope.   It is the secret that moves
with the speed of life,
    secrets of night and   the street
secrets of milk and dinner and daylight,
enigmas of gardens, the kitchen and the bed,
the riddle and sacrament in the knot of wood,
in the wine, in the water and root the coil of life.

They ask for answers, they starving eat their shadows.
The beginning is always here.   Its green demand.

V

They think I answer and strangle.   They are wrong.
I set my life among the questioning.
The peasant, the wars, the wounded powerful king.
The shining of questions which cannot be concealed
lies in that mirror.   The little child to the mother
of the father's unspoken death, said   :   "You have told me
    yourself."
Even alone, away from daily life, the fire
and monster crown of the legend over me
reaches their eyes   —   children, friendship of lions,
the sense of the world at last broken through to man
in all fury, all sacred open mystery,
is in my question.
                    The stranger, the foreign and strong,
 the child and king, wide village eyes of the farm,
the demand loud, or choking in surf-foam,
density of flowers, the faces of all love,
the core of our hope;   stronger than kill,
stronger almost than question, almost than song.

ELEGY IN JOY

TENTH ELEGY.   ELEGY IN JOY

Now green, now burning, I make a way for peace.
After the green and long beyond my lake,
among those fields of people, on these illuminated
hills, gold, burnt gold, spilled gold and shadowed blue,
the light of enormous flame, the flowing light of the sea,
where all the lights and nights are reconciled.
The sea at last, where all the waters lead.
And all the wars to this peace.

For the sea does not lie like the death you imagine;
this sea is the real sea, here it is.
This is the living.   This peace is the face of the world,
a fierce angel who in one lifetime lives
fighting a lifetime, dying as we all die,
becoming forever, the continual god.

Years of our time, this heart!   The binding of the alone,
bells of all loneliness, binding our lands and our music,
branches full of motion each opening its own flower,
lands of all song, each speaking in his own voice.
Praise in every grace
among the old same war.

Years of betrayal, million death breeding its weaknesses
and hope, buried more deep more black than dream.
Every elegy is the present :   freedom eating our hearts,
death and explosion, and the world unbegun.
Now burning and unbegun, I sing earth with its war,
and God the future, and the wish of man.

•

Though you die, your war lives :   the years fought it,
fusing a dead world straight.

The living will be giving you your meanings,
widening to love because of the love of man.
All the wounds crying
I feare, and hope : I burne, and frese like yse . . .
saying to the beloved
For your sake I love cities,
on your love I love the many,
saying to the people,
for your sake I love the world.
The old wounds crying
I find no peace, and all my warres are done.

> Out of our life the living eyes
> See peace in our own image made,
> Able to give only what we can give:
> Bearing two days like midnight.   "Live,"
> The moment offers;   the night requires
> Promise effort love and praise.

Now there are no maps and no magicians.
No prophets but the young prophet, the sense of the world.
The gift of our time, the world to be discovered.
All the continents giving off their several lights,
the one sea, and the air.   And all things glow.

Move as this sea moves, as water, as force.
Peace shines from its life, its war can become
at any moment the fierce shining of peace,
and all the life-night long many voices are saying
The name of all things is Glowing.

A beginning, a moment of rest that imagines.
And again I go wandering far and alone,
I rise at night, I start up in the silence—
lovely and silver-black the night remembers.
In the cities of America I make my peace;
among the bombs and commands,
the sound that war makes
NO   NO
We see their weeping and their lifetime dreams.

All this, they say to us, because of you.
Much to begin.   Now be your green, your burning,
bear also our joy, come to our meeting-place
and in the triumph of the reconceived
lie down at last together face to face.

•

We tell beginnings :   for the flesh and answer,
for the look, the lake in the eye that knows,
for the despair that flows down in widest rivers,
cloud of home;   and also the green tree of grace,
all in the leaf, in the love that gives us ourselves.

The word of nourishment passes through the women,
soldiers and orchards rooted in constellations,
white towers, eyes of children:
saying in time of war What shall we feed?
I cannot say the end.

Nourish beginnings, let us nourish beginnings.
Not all things are blest, but the
seeds of all things are blest.
The blessing is in the seed.

This moment, this seed, this wave of the sea, this look, this instant
    of love.
Years over wars and an imagining of peace.   Or the expiation
    journey
toward peace which is many wishes flaming together,
fierce pure life, the many-living home.
Love that gives us ourselves, in the world known to all
new techniques for the healing of a wound,
and the unknown world.   One life, or the faring stars.

NINE POEMS

NINE POEMS

for the unborn child

I

The childless years alone without a home
Flashed daily with the world's glimpse, happiness.
Always behind was the dark screen of loss
Hardly moving, like heavy hardly-moving cloud.
"Give me myself," or "Take me," I said aloud;
There was little to give, and always less to take.
Except the promise, except the promise darkness
Makes, night and daylight, miracle to come.

Flying over, I suddenly saw the traces
Of man : where man is, you may read the wind
In shadow and smoke, know how the wind is gone
And know the way of man;   in the fall of the plane
Into its levels, encounter the ancient spaces:
The fall to life, the cliff and strait of bone.

II

They came to me and said, "There is a child."
Fountains of images broke through my land.
My swords, my fountains spouted past my eyes
And in my flesh at last I saw.   Returned
To when we drove in the high forest, and earth
Turned to glass in the sunset where the wild
Trees struck their roots as deep and visible
As their high branches, the double planted world.

"There is no father," they came and said to me.
— I have known fatherless children, the searching, walk
The world, look at all faces for their father's life.
Their choice is death or the world.   And they do choose.
Earn their brave set of bone, the seeking marvelous look
Of those who lose and use and know their lives.

III

There is a place.   There is a miracle.
I know the nightmare, the black and bone piano,
The statues in the kitchen, a house dissolving in air.
I know the lilac-turreted cathedral
Taking its roots from willows that changed before my eyes
When all became real, real as the sound of bells.
We earthly are aware of transformation;
Miraculously, life, from the old despair.

The wave of smooth water approaches on the sea-
Surface, a live wave individual
Linking, massing its color.   Moving, is struck by wind,
Ribbed, steepened, until the slope and ridge begin;
Comes nearer, brightens.   Now curls, its vanishing
Hollows darken and disappear;   now high above
Me, the scroll, froth, foam of the overfall.

IV

Now the ideas all change to animals
Loping and gay, now all the images
Transform to leaves, now all these screens of leaves
Are flowing into rivers, I am in love
With rivers, these changing waters carry voices,
Carry all children;   carry all delight.
The water-soothed winds move warm above these waves.
The child changes and moves among these waves.

The waves are changing, they tremble from waves of waters
To other essentials — they become waves of light
And wander through my sleep and through my waking,
And through my hands and over my lips and over
Me;   brilliant and transformed and clear,
The pure light.   Now I am light and nothing more.

V

Eating sleep, eating sunlight, eating meat,
Lying in the sun to stare
At deliverance, the rapid cloud,
Gull-wing opposing sun-bright wind,
I see the born who dare
Walk on green, walk against blue,
Move in the nightlong flare
Of love on darkness, traveling
Among the rings of light to simple light,
From nowhere to nowhere.
And in my body feel the seasons grow.
Who is it in the dim room?   Who is there?

VI

Death's threat!   Today I have known laughter
As if for the first time;   have seen into your eyes,
Death, past the still gaze, and found two I love.
One chose you gladly with a laugh advancing,
His hands full of guns, on the enemy in Spain.
The other living with the choice of life
Turning each day of living to the living day.
The strength, the grossness, spirit and gall of choice.

They came to me and said, "If you must choose,
Is it yourself or the child?"   Laughter I learned
In that moment, laughter and choice of life.
I saw an immense ship trembling on the water
Lift by a gesture of hands.   I saw a child.   I saw
A red room, the eyes, the hands, the hands and eyes.

VII

You will enter the world where death by fear and explosion
Is waited;   longed for by many;   by all dreamed.
You will enter the world where various poverty
Makes thin the imagination and the bone.
You will enter the world where birth is walled about,
Where years are walled journeys, death a walled-in act.
You will enter the world which eats itself
Naming faith, reason, naming love, truth, fact.

You in your dark lake moving darkly now
Will leave a house that time makes, times to come
Enter the present, where all the deaths and all
The old betrayals have come home again.
World where again Judas, the little child,
May grow and choose.   You will enter the world.

VIII

Child who within me gives me dreams and sleep,
Your sleep, your dreams;   you hold me in your flesh
Including me where nothing has included
Until I said   :   I will include, will wish
And in my belly be a birth, will keep
All delicacy, all delight unclouded.

Dreams of an unborn child move through my dreams,
The sun is not alone in making fire and wave
Find meeting-place, for flesh and future meet,
The seal in the green wave like you in me,
Child.   My blood at night full of your dreams,
Sleep coming by day as strong as sun on me,
Coming with sun-dreams where leaves and rivers meet,
And I at last alive sunlight and wave.

IX

Rider of dream, the body as an image
Alone in crisis.   I have seen the wind,
Its tall cloud standing on a pillar of air,
The toe of the whirlwind turning on the ground.
Have known in myself hollow bodiless shade,
The shadow falling from the tree to the ground,
Have lost and lost and now at last am found
For a moment of sleep and waking, striking root.

Praise that the homeless may in their bodies be
A house that time makes, where the future moves
In his dark lake.   Praise that the cities of men,
The fields of men, may at all moments choose.
Lose, use, and live.   And at this daylight, praise
To the grace of the world and time that I may hope
To live, to write, to see my human child.